Stark County District Library
www.StarkLibrary.org
330.452.0665

FEB   2013

D1466228

How to Analyze the Works of

JOHN
ADAMS

by Maggie Combs

ABDO
Publishing Company

Essential Critiques

How to Analyze the Works of

JOHN
ADAMS

by Maggie Combs

Content Consultant: Dr. Ryan Lee Teten
Assistant Professor and Anthony Moroux/BORSF Professor of Political Science,
University of Louisiana

Credits

Published by ABDO Publishing Company, PO Box 398166, Minneapolis, MN 55439. Copyright © 2013 by Abdo Consulting Group, Inc. International copyrights reserved in all countries. No part of this book may be reproduced in any form without written permission from the publisher. The Essential Library™ is a trademark and logo of ABDO Publishing Company.

Printed in the United States of America,
North Mankato, Minnesota
102012
012013

 THIS BOOK CONTAINS AT LEAST 10% RECYCLED MATERIALS.

Editor: Sarah Frigon
Series Designer: Marie Tupy

Cataloging-in-Publication Data
Combs, Maggie.
 How to analyze the works of John Adams / Maggie Combs.
   p. cm. -- (Essential critiques)
Includes bibliographical references and index.
ISBN 978-1-61783-646-6
1. Adams, John--1735-1826--Criticism and interpretation--Juvenile literature.
2. Presidents--United States--Juvenile literature. 3. Speeches, addresses, etc.,
American--Juvenile literature. I. Title.
973.8--dc14

2012946165

Table of Contents

1

Introduction to Critiques

What Is Critical Theory?

What do you usually do when you read a book or essay or listen to a speech? You probably absorb the specific language style of the work. You also consider the point the speaker or writer is trying to convey. Yet these are only a few of many possible ways of understanding and appreciating a speech or piece of writing. What if you are interested in delving more deeply? You might want to learn more about the writer or speaker and how his or her personal background is reflected in the work. Or you might want to examine what the work says about society—how it depicts the roles of women and minorities, for example. If so, you have entered the realm of critical theory.

The end.

Critical theory helps you learn how art, literature, music, theater, film, politics, and other endeavors either support or challenge the way society behaves. Critical theory is the evaluation and interpretation of a work using different philosophies, or schools of thought. Critical theory can be used to understand all types of cultural works.

There are many different critical theories. Each theory asks you to look at the work from a different perspective. Some theories address social issues, while others focus on the writer's or speaker's life or the time period in which the work was created. For example, the critical theory that asks how an author's life affected the work is called biographical criticism. Other common schools of criticism include historical criticism, feminist criticism, psychological criticism, and New Criticism, which examines a work solely within the context of the work itself.

What Is the Purpose of Critical Theory?

Critical theory can open your mind to new ways of thinking. It can help you evaluate a piece of writing or a speech from a new perspective, directing your attention to issues and messages you may not otherwise recognize in a work. For example, applying feminist criticism to an essay may make you aware of female stereotypes perpetuated in the work. Applying a critical theory to a speech helps you learn about the person who gave it or the society that heard it. You can also explore how the work is perceived by current cultures.

How Do You Apply Critical Theory?

You conduct a critique when you use a critical theory to examine and question a work. The theory you choose is a lens through which you can view the work, or a springboard for asking questions about the work. Applying a critical theory helps you think critically about the work. You are free to question the work and make assertions about it. If you choose to examine an essay using biographical criticism, for example, you want to know how the writer's personal background or education inspired or shaped the work. You could explore why the writer was drawn to the subject. For instance, are there any parallels between points raised in the essay and details from the writer's life?

Forming a Thesis

Ask your question and find answers in the work or other related materials. Then you can create a thesis. The thesis is the key point in your critique. It is your argument about the work based on the tenets, or beliefs, of the theory you are using. For example, if you are using biographical criticism to ask how the writer's life inspired the work, your thesis could be worded as follows: Writer Teng Xiong, raised in refugee camps in Southeast Asia, drew upon her experiences to write the essay "No Home for Me."

> ### How to Make a Thesis Statement
>
> In a critique, a thesis statement typically appears at the end of the introductory paragraph. It is usually only one sentence long and states the author's main idea.

Providing Evidence

Once you have formed a thesis, you must provide evidence to support it. Evidence might take the form of examples and quotations from the work itself—such as excerpts from an essay. Articles about the essay or personal interviews with the writer might also support your ideas. You may wish to address what other critics have written about the work. Quotes from these individuals may help support your claim. If you find any quotes or examples that contradict your thesis, you will need to create an argument against them. For instance: <u>Many critics have pointed to the essay "No Home for Me" as detailing only the powerless circumstances Xiong faced. However, in the paragraphs focused on her emigration to the United States, Xiong clearly depicts herself as someone who can shape her own future.</u>

How to Support a Thesis Statement

A critique should include several arguments. Arguments support a thesis claim. An argument is one or two sentences long and is supported by evidence from the work being discussed.

Organize the arguments into paragraphs. These paragraphs make up the body of the critique.

In This Book

In this book, you will read summaries of famous works by President John Adams, each followed by a critique. Each critique will use one theory and apply it to one work. Critical thinking sections will give you a chance to consider other theses and questions about the work. Did you agree with the author's application of the theory? What other questions are raised by the thesis and its arguments? You can also find out what other critics think about each work. Then, in the You Critique It section in the final pages of this book, you will have an opportunity to create your own critique.

Look for the Guides

Throughout the chapters that analyze the works, thesis statements have been highlighted. The box next to the thesis helps explain what questions are being raised about the work. Supporting arguments have been underlined. The boxes next to the arguments help explain how these points support the thesis. Look for these guides throughout each critique.

Essential Critiques

Even before he was president, John Adams played an influential role in the founding of the United States.

2

A Closer Look at John Adams

Family Life

John Adams was born on October 30, 1735, to a Massachusetts farmer, also named John Adams, and his wife Susanna. John's father served in various capacities in the local militia and was an active member in the local government. The Adamses were an established colonial family. Their homestead had been founded in Braintree, Massachusetts, in 1639, and the family could trace a maternal ancestor back to the Plymouth Colony. John was the eldest of three boys who all learned hard work and a commitment to public life from their highly religious parents.

John's father wanted his son to become a minister. In 1755, John attended Harvard in pursuit of his father's dream, but he would never lead a congregation. Instead, John taught grammar school for a few years before beginning a law practice in Boston in 1758. He married a minister's daughter, Abigail Smith, on October 25, 1764. Together they raised one daughter and three sons, losing another daughter during infancy.

Abigail proved a great asset to John when he entered political life. He was hot-tempered and opinionated; she was steady and resolute. They had an unusually close and interdependent relationship that later generations have come to admire. An extensive collection of their intimate letters has been preserved as a national treasure. John's political life would take him away from their home for long periods of time, and the couple was never happy with the separation. "I can do nothing without you," John often told Abigail in his letters.[1] His reliance on Abigail made her nearly as influential a person in the American Revolution as her husband.

Before the Revolution

In 1765, shortly after his marriage to Abigail, Adams wrote a series of articles published as *A Dissertation on the Canon and Feudal Law*. These articles protested the Stamp Act, a tax Great Britain placed on certain goods sold in the colonies. The articles launched Adams into a prominent public role through his strong opposition to the act. When the British government created the Townshend Acts in 1767 to tax goods imported to the colonies, Adams led the opposition.

Adams was also a character of controversy leading up to the American Revolution (1775–1783). He put his principles before his politics. When a group of British soldiers opened fire on colonists during the Boston Massacre of 1770, Adams acted as a defense lawyer for the soldiers. He believed they were innocent because they had been provoked to fire. This was the first of many instances in which Adams would follow his principles rather than popular opinion. At times, his insistence on following his own beliefs and principles made him very unpopular.

Revolutionary

The people of Massachusetts elected Adams as a delegate to the First Continental Congress in 1774. This Congress was convened to determine a response to the Intolerable Acts, a series of laws passed by the British government that triggered outrage in the American colonies. Adams attended along with his cousin, Samuel Adams, who is known as the Father of the American Revolution. Together they opposed reconciliation with Great Britain despite other colonists' strong support for cooperation with the British government.

When Adams was elected as a delegate to the Second Continental Congress in 1775, he already had a reputation as a revolutionary. This time, recent events would play to his advantage. Further problems with Great Britain, including violence between American colonists and British troops, had convinced a majority of the delegates to call for independence. Adams played a key role on the committee to draft the declaration and supported his friend, writer and politician Thomas Jefferson, as the author. After the declaration had been written, Adams led the debate in favor of Jefferson's draft. The Second Continental Congress approved the Declaration of Independence on July 4, 1776.

Adams played several other important roles in the American Revolution during his time with the Second Continental Congress. He nominated George Washington as general of the colonial army.

He helped create the country's navy and had a large influence on all the workings of the Congress, serving as head of 25 committees. In 1778, the Congress sent Adams to France to negotiate a war alliance. Soon afterward, he returned home and drafted the Massachusetts state constitution in 1780. That constitution would become the model for all other state constitutions and would have a prominent influence on the Constitution of the United States.

The Adams homestead is now a national historical park in Quincy, Massachusetts.

Founding Father

Adams continued his political career as the country's ambassador to Paris, France, with Benjamin Franklin in 1780. In 1785, he became the first American ambassador to the British court. During this time, he wrote *A Defence of the Constitutions of Government of the United States of America*, his response to the arguments surrounding the country's new Constitution.

After returning to his Braintree homestead in 1788, Adams received the second-most votes in the country's first election and became the first vice president of the United States. Although vice president was mostly a title with little responsibility, Adams supported all of Washington's major initiatives. After serving as vice president from 1789 to 1797, Adams was elected as the second president of the United States. He won the 1796 election against Thomas Jefferson by only three electoral votes, giving Adams the presidency and Jefferson the vice presidency. Adams was a member of the Federalist Party, which favored a strong central government, while Jefferson was a member of the Democratic-Republican Party, which favored a government with limited powers. Adams's inaugural address of March 4, 1797, aimed to unite the country behind him.

During his time in office, Adams was a controversial figure. He often went against the advice of his cabinet. Instead of siding with Great Britain in the country's conflict with France, he sent peace delegations to France to avoid throwing the United States into war. His presidency reached its lowest popularity after he signed the Alien and Sedition Acts of 1798, which allowed the government to deport those born in foreign countries and arrest newspaper writers and editors who criticized the government. In 1800, Jefferson defeated Adams in his bid for a second term, ending his presidency.

Although political rivalries had pitted the old friends against each other in several elections, Adams and Jefferson renewed their friendship through an extensive correspondence during their retirement. They died within hours of each other on July 4, 1826, the fiftieth anniversary of the Declaration of Independence. Adams's death on this date was a fitting end for a man who had devoted his life to securing and preserving the ideals of the Declaration of Independence.

Abigail Adams was Adams's most trusted adviser in both political and domestic matters.

An Overview of Adams's Writings on Women's Right to Vote

Historical Context

Women in pre- and post-Revolutionary America held much less influence in politics and government than they do today. Women typically ran the family and home and assisted in the household business, which was usually farming or a trade. Girls learned the skills necessary to manage a household from their mothers while their brothers were usually apprenticed to a local tradesman. Only upper-class girls received any education outside of the home, and even then they were not allowed to attend universities. Although women held power in the home, they had little within the government. Some women were allowed to vote in elections early in the foundation of the nation, but this right disappeared after the first few federal elections.

The women's suffrage movement did not gain momentum in the United States until the mid-nineteenth century. However, conversations about women's right to vote began much earlier. Adams's contributions to the conversation were recorded in several letters. One was a letter he wrote to his wife, Abigail Adams, on April 14, 1776. Adams also addressed the issue in a letter to James Sullivan, a Massachusetts judge, written on May 26, 1776. Adams's letters provide a glimpse into the conflicting currents within society at the time of the American Revolution.

Abigail's Letter

Adams wrote his April 14 letter in response to a letter from Abigail from March 31. The main body of Abigail's letter describes her return to their home in Boston after the successful siege of the British-held city by American troops. She tells him, "I long to hear that you have declared an independency."[1] While she writes, Adams is attending the Second Continental Congress, during which Jefferson would pen the Declaration of Independence. The Declaration would be published on July 4, 1776. In her letter, Abigail tells Adams, "By the way in the new Code of Laws which I suppose it will be necessary for you to make" following the proclaiming of independence, "I desire you would Remember the Ladies."[2] The colonies were preparing to rebel against Great Britain. Many colonists were unhappy because they did not have a say in the government or their taxation. Abigail points out that, "If particular care and attention is not paid to the Ladies we are determined to foment a Rebellion, and will not hold ourselves bound by any Laws in which we have no voice, or Representation."[3] In other words, if women are not counted as equals and are not involved in making the laws that affect them, they may also rebel. "That your Sex are Naturally Tyrannical is a Truth so thoroughly established as to admit of no dispute," she tells him, "but such of you as wish to be happy willingly give up the harsh title of Master for the more tender and endearing one of Friend."[4] She concludes by asking him to not forget that women are the men's God-given helpers and that "Men of Sense in all Ages abhor those customs which treat us only as the vassals of your Sex."[5] In other words, if Adams is a sensible man, he will see the justice in her request.

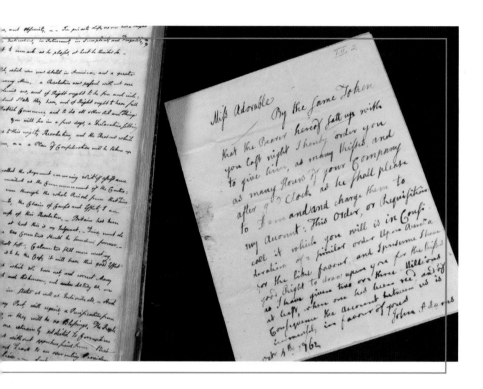

Throughout the course of their lives together, Adams and Abigail wrote thousands of letters to each other.

Though only part of her letter is spent on this request, it was not a light one. This letter is considered one of the benchmarks of the movement for women's rights. With such an influential woman pleading the case, it would be heard.

Adams's Response

Adams's response begins by detailing the current state of the army. He also replies to Abigail's concerns about the slow progress of declaring independence and her comments about the state of the colonies. At the end, Adams addresses her request to "Remember the Ladies." He responds with humor, saying he "cannot but laugh."[6] Adams tells her, "Our Struggle has loosened the bands of Government every where," and the Second Continental Congress has been warned that declaring independence will create rebellions by children, apprentices, Native Americans, and even African-American slaves. But her letter was the first time Adams had heard that women, who are "more numerous and powerfull than all the rest," were discontent.[7]

Adams assures Abigail that men are the masters in name only; in practice, they are truly the subjects of the women around them. "We dare not exert our Power in its full Latitude," he states. "We are obliged to go fair, and softly."[8] He then proposes the supporters of the monarchy are inciting groups, including women, to threaten rebellion in order to keep the Continental Congress from declaring independence. It is impossible to know the true intent of Abigail's original letter and Adams's response, but it is clear the subject of women's right to vote was a topic of discussion in even the highest political circles in the country.

Adams to James Sullivan, May 26, 1776

Adams wrote his letter to James Sullivan in response to Sullivan's letter on the issue of voting rights in the colonies. At the time, Sullivan was a member of the Massachusetts Supreme Court and Adams was Massachusetts's delegate to the Continental Congress. Sullivan hoped to expand voting rights, but Adams was more cautious.

Adams tells Sullivan he agrees the "moral Foundation of Government is the Consent of the People."[9] However, Adams disagrees with how Sullivan applies this principle. In Sullivan's earlier letter, he had argued that all men should have the right to vote, while at the time only men over the age of 21 who owned property had that right.

Adams argues that if men who do not own property are given the right to vote, arguments no longer exist against giving women and children the right to vote as well. In his opinion, a man without property does not have experience applicable to understanding government, any more than a woman whose life is spent in the care of children does. According to Adams, men "who are wholly destitute of Property, are also too little acquainted with public Affairs to form a Right Judgment."[10]

As a result, they are easily swayed by men who would seek to influence them.

Adams attributes this principle to the concept that "Power always follows Property."[11] He then argues that instead of giving all men the right to vote, the government should focus on making it easier to own land, thereby imparting the wisdom required to vote. Adams also reminds Sullivan the people of Massachusetts have always only allowed men with land to vote, and they are not interested in changing this law now.

Sullivan had suggested that all men be allowed to vote on any laws that would affect the life and liberty of all but not on the laws that would affect only men who own land. Again, Adams reminds Sullivan that using this logic would lead to allowing both women and children the right to vote. He also reminds Sullivan that women and children may have "as good Judgment, and as independent Minds as those Men who are wholly destitute of property."[12] Adams concludes by admitting that some women, children, and men without property have enough knowledge to vote. However, the government must apply the general rule to all to avoid chaos.

Abigail Adams is memorialized as a pioneer in women's rights at the Boston Women's Memorial.

How to Apply Feminist Criticism to Adams's Writings on Women's Right to Vote

What Is Feminist Criticism?

Feminism is the belief women should have the same rights and opportunities as men. Feminist criticism was born during the women's movement in the 1960s. This type of criticism most often focuses on the study and promotion of works created by women, or on critiquing depictions of women in works created by men. Feminist criticism may also analyze works by women to determine if or how stereotypes prevalent in the culture appear in these works.

The attitudes about women prevalent in a culture may change over time. Also, different groups within the same culture may hold contradictory beliefs. Both of these aspects may be taken into account by the feminist criticism of a work.

There are several major questions feminists use to approach literature. How does the work represent and promote patriarchy? How does the work demonstrate the author's view of women? What female stereotypes does this work perpetuate? What does the work say about the intersection of womanhood and race, class, and other cultural factors?

Applying Feminist Criticism to Adams's Writings on Women's Right to Vote

Adams supported the revolution to gain independence from Great Britain and to form a free government with free elections. However, he did not plan to extend women the right to vote under the new government. He explains his reasoning in letters to his wife, Abigail Adams, and to Massachusetts judge James Sullivan. Despite Adams's respect for his wife and his views on freedom, he perpetuates the prevailing views of his culture through his political stance that women should not be allowed to vote.

Thesis Statement

At the end of the first paragraph, the author states the thesis: "Despite Adams's respect for his wife and his views on freedom, he perpetuates the prevailing views of his culture through his political stance that women should not be allowed to vote." A feminist thesis will always focus on how women are affected by the work being critiqued.

<u>Adams's letters demonstrate how his society as a whole viewed women.</u> During the time, the role of most women was limited in many respects. In the letter Adams wrote to Sullivan on May 26, 1776, he references what he believes to be their shared views on women. In response to Sullivan's request to extend the right to vote to men without property, Adams poses the question, "But why exclude Women?"[1]

> **Argument One**
> The first argument is: "Adams's letters demonstrate how his society as a whole viewed women." This sets up ideas the author will reference throughout the critique.

Adams then acts out Sullivan's part in the argument, writing, "Their Delicacy renders them unfit for Practice and Experience, in the great Business of Life, and the hardy Enterprises of War, as well as the arduous Cares of State." He adds, "Besides, their attention is So much engaged with the necessary Nurture of their Children, that Nature has made them fittest for domestic Cares."[2] This statement makes it clear Adams's worldview was in step with society's at the time, which held that women were the weaker sex.

<u>Although Adams trusted Abigail to help him make even his most difficult political decisions, he</u>

Argument Two

The second argument states: "Although Adams trusted Abigail to help him make even his most difficult political decisions, he did not extend his high opinion of her to all women." In this paragraph, the author demonstrates the contrast between Adams's attitude toward his wife and in his beliefs about women as a group.

<u>did not extend his high opinion of her to all women.</u> Because of Adams's political career, he was often absent, which meant raising the children and managing the household were left entirely to Abigail. Historians view Abigail as Adams's chief adviser in all matters, including politics. Even politicians at the time recognized Abigail's influence on Adams was so strong she was practically a politician herself. Adams himself called Abigail "My Dearest friend."[3] He referred to her as "my dear Partner . . . to take part with me in the struggle."[4] He even called her his "wisest friend in the world."[5] However, when it came to women's voting rights, Adams was not willing to expand that privilege to the rest of the women in the colonies.

In his letter to Sullivan, Adams states, "Society can be governed only by general Rules. Government cannot accommodate itself to every particular Case, as it happens, nor to the Circumstances of particular Persons."[6] As a result, even if certain individuals of a group have the understanding of politics necessary

to vote, the right should not be extended to all.
By similar logic, if the vote were extended to men
without property, it would then have to be extended
to women and children. This echoes Adams's letter
to Abigail. The Second Continental Congress had
been warned if they declared independence from
Great Britain it would cause other minority groups
to rise up, who might then also desire the right
to vote.

Although Adams believed
in independence from Great
Britain, he failed to apply that
ideal to the minority classes.
In Abigail's letter to Adams
on March 31, 1776, she asks
him to "Remember the Ladies"
as he works as part of the
Continental Congress to declare

> **Argument Three**
> The final argument states:
> "Although Adams believed
> in independence from Great
> Britain, he failed to apply that
> ideal to the minority classes."
> This section emphasizes the
> contradictions that can arise
> when groups are excluded
> from consideration.

independence from Great Britain and to establish a
new form of government.[7] In his reply to Abigail,
Adams tells her the members of the revolution had
been warned their own revolution might lead to
the uprisings of children, servants, students, Native
Americans, and slaves. But Adams is surprised by
the idea that their revolution could lead to a revolt

by women as well. He had not applied the ideals of independence and freedom to anyone beyond white male property owners. Abigail, on the other hand, saw the new government as an opportunity to increase women's rights as well.

Conclusion

The last paragraph of the critique serves as a conclusion. The first few sentences summarize the thesis and arguments. The last sentence ties the ideas presented in the critique together and projects their effects into the future.

Adams was a strong voice in the United States' fight for freedom, but he did not carry that ideal over into extending rights for women. He shared his society's general views of women as a group. Though he depended on his wife Abigail's opinion on everything from domestic cares to politics, he did not feel it was prudent to expand the right to vote to everyone. As a result of this and similar attitudes during the founding of the nation, women did not receive the right to vote in the United States until the Nineteenth Amendment was passed in 1919.

Thinking Critically about Adams's Writings on Women's Right to Vote

Now it is your turn to assess the critique. Think about these questions:

1. Feminist criticism addresses the use of stereotypes. What stereotypes about women are described in this essay?

2. Feminist criticism focuses on how women are portrayed in works by both women and men. How does Abigail's letter portray women? In what ways does it reflect the culture of the time?

3. What was the most convincing argument the author made? What was the weakest? Why?

Other Approaches

One feminist critique of Adams's letters is presented in the essay above. However, a feminist critique of these letters does not have to focus on the time in which Adams lived. Another essay might focus on the joking tone of the letters of Adams and Abigail. Yet another thesis could discuss Adams's failure to address the voting rights of a woman who owns property.

Wedded Words

In Adams's letter responding to Abigail's request on behalf of women, Adams says he "cannot but laugh" and calls her original comments "saucy."[8] Rather than disregarding Abigail's concerns in his response, he may be replying in kind, using the same tone she used in her letter. It is possible there are undercurrents in the letters that were clear to the couple but not to another reader. A thesis statement for an essay studying this concept might be: In his letter to Abigail on April 14, 1776, Adams replies to the tone of Abigail's original request rather than its message.

Women Who Own Are Overlooked

The arguments in Adams's letter to Sullivan on May 26, 1776, focus on only allowing men who own property to vote. Adams asserts that it takes the knowledge gained by owning and managing property to make an informed vote. This argument overlooks the fact that unmarried women in colonial America were allowed to own property. A thesis for this essay would state: Adams's arguments for limiting the right to vote to those who own property overlooked women who own property, revealing a bias that reflected his society's views on women.

Essential Critiques

Adams, *center*, served as the first US ambassador to Great Britain and its king, George III, *right*.

5

An Overview of the Preface to *A Defence of the Constitutions of Government of the United States of America*

Historical Context

Adams wrote the three volumes of *A Defence of the Constitutions of Government of the United States of America* while serving as the first US ambassador to Great Britain after the American Revolution. While Adams was overseas, the Constitutional Convention wrote a new Constitution of the United States. Not all states responded positively to the new Constitution because it gave states fewer rights while making the federal government more powerful. It would have been difficult for an outspoken man like Adams to stay out of the political discussion, even while outside the country. The publication of *A Defence of the Constitutions of Government of the United States of America* in 1787 added his support.

A Heartfelt Defense

In the first volume, Adams explores both modern and ancient governments. Adams uses the preface to promote a government based on reason and to argue that a republic is the strongest form of government. His argument was based on a European philosophical movement known as the Enlightenment. The major principles of the Enlightenment were reason, the scientific method, and the empowerment of people to create a perfect society. Philosophers of the Enlightenment critiqued and applied reason to the social institutions of their day, including religion.

Adams begins the preface by arguing the European monarchies have become more like republics. Most of the monarchies of his time included aspects of republics, giving citizens power to influence laws and protecting religious freedom, security of property, personal liberty, freedom of press, freedom of commerce, and the right to a public trial. Despite these new freedoms under European monarchies, only the governments of Great Britain and the United States used separation of powers and checks and balances.

To Adams, two uses of the separation of powers are essential for a successful government. The first is the separation of executive, legislative, and judicial powers. The executive branch, which includes the president of the United States, is responsible for carrying out the laws. Congress is part of the legislative branch, which makes the laws. And the judicial branch includes the court system, from local courts to the Supreme Court, the highest court in the land. In this system, each branch is able to keep other branches in check by having power over some of their processes.

The second aspect of separation of powers occurs in the legislative branch. Adams believed it was best to break Congress into two different parts: a House of Representatives and a Senate. The number of votes a state has in the House of Representatives is based on its population, while each state has two votes in the Senate. As laws worked through both parts of Congress, they would be made slowly with serious thought coming from both the House and the Senate. The end goal of the checks and balances in a republican government is "the sense of the people, the public voice."[1]

Objectionable Governments

Adams describes ancient Greece as another example of a democracy. However, unlike the United States, it was without the checks and balances of executive, legislative, and judicial branches. As a result, people used the name of democracy to take revenge on their personal enemies. According to the Greek historian Thucydides, nearly 60,000 people were killed and 20,000 banished from Greece to defend the democracy. According to Adams, by this evidence, the democracy of Greece was inferior to the republic of the United States.

After addressing democracy in Greece, Adams notes the pitfalls of monarchy. Kings have nobles to keep them in check, but both are power hungry, so the check does not work for long. If the kings did not have armies to support their position, the nobles would overturn the monarchy and rule in its place. According to Adams, it is popular to say that if the monarch were guaranteed to be wise and moral, a simple monarchy would be the best form of government. Adams does not agree. The judicial and legislative branches of a republican government help a wise and moral king better govern his people.

A king can never know the needs of his people as well as the representatives of a legislative branch can. Adams concludes his arguments against other forms of government by stating,

> *If there is one certain truth to be collected*
> *from the history of all ages, it is this: That*
> *the people's rights and liberties, and the*
> *democratical mixture in a constitution, can*
> *never be preserved . . . without separating*
> *the executive power from the legislative.*[2]

Divine Right

Adams then recounts the history of the use of divine right to support government. Although the term *divine right* originated in Europe, Adams highlights evidence of the belief much further back in time. He notes the laws of Crete were said to have been given by the god Jupiter, the laws of Lacedaemon by the god Apollo, and the Roman laws by the god Egeria. Scandinavia attributed its government to the gods Woden and Thor. The Inca of Peru believed their first ruler was a god. Some Native Americans believed their chiefs to be under the protection of the god War.

The government of the United States of America stands in contrast to the concept of divine right. Instead of being based on the authority of a God-given leader, according to Adams, the US government was founded on the "simple principles of nature . . . by the use of reason and the senses."[3] The writers of the Constitution considered law to be part of the arts and sciences. Adams accuses past governments that established laws based on divine right of being without honor and without respect for their citizens. The Constitution, in contrast, is "grounded on reason, morality, and the Christian religion."[4]

Roman Philosophers

Adams finishes his preface by explaining how the writings of two Roman philosophers, Tacitus and Cicero, support a republican government. Tacitus supported a system of checks and balances between the three branches of government. Only a few fragments of books written by Tacitus survived until the time of the American Revolution, but Adams strongly agrees with the few excerpts that remain. Adams asserts the book was focused upon how checks and balances are the "strongest anchor

Tacitus was a Roman philosopher who supported a system of checks and balances.

of safety to the community."[5] Adams turns next to Cicero, whom Adams believed to be the greatest politician and philosopher who ever lived. Cicero believed reason would lead to a government of three branches. From this evidence, Adams asserts that if Cicero and Tacitus were alive, they would completely support the creation of a republican government through the Constitution of the United States.

Adams was strongly influenced by the Age of Enlightenment and the philosophers whose ideas were at its foundation.

How to Apply Religious Criticism to the Preface to *A Defence of the Constitutions of Government of the United States of America*

What Is Religious Criticism?

Religious criticism addresses two human needs: the need for academic information and the desire for spiritual growth. It is closely related to moral and ethical criticism, which critique how a work teaches its audience principles and values. Religious criticism can focus on how a work treats and defines religion and spirituality. Religious criticism looks at how spirituality is part of all art, whether the artist includes it intentionally or unintentionally.

While religion was once a standard lens people used to view the world, the language of religion has become a lesser part of today's discourse. Religious critics seek to bring religion and spirituality back into the academic discussion by answering some of the following questions: How does this work reflect the religion of a culture? Do the characters or themes of this work have a spiritual dimension? How does this work address and define religion? Is the need for spirituality reflected intentionally or unintentionally through this work?

Applying Religious Criticism to the Preface to *A Defence of the Constitutions of Government of the United States of America*

Although the power of the monarchies was beginning to fade in Europe in the late eighteenth century, the new government in the colonies faced its own challenges. In the preface to *A Defence of the Constitutions of Government of the United States of America*, Adams rejects divine right as a basis for a government's authority. Instead, he insists that reason, a key principle of the Enlightenment, will support a stable republican government. Adams uses the authority of reason, not religion, to establish a republican government as the best form of government.

Thesis Statement

The main argument of this essay is stated in its thesis: "Adams uses the authority of reason, not religion, to establish a republican government as the best form of government." This thesis sets up the conflict between reason and divine right.

In the preface, Adams criticizes other governments' reliance on the concept of divine right to establish rulers and the power of the government. Adams rejects this concept, contending it uses established religious beliefs to enable a leader to seize power and gain people's obedience. Adams's main point is that if the power of a god must be invoked to keep citizens from rebelling, the form of government falls short. Adams does not criticize religion when he criticizes the idea of divine right. In fact, in the preface he describes the government of the United States as a government "grounded on reason, morality, and the Christian religion."[1] He argues against the misuse of religion and religious ideals rather than against religion itself. Although Enlightenment thinkers critiqued religion, they regarded it as a significant part of society.

Adams appeals directly to his fellow Americans' reason in

Argument One

The first argument states: "In the preface, Adams criticizes other governments' reliance on the concept of divine right to establish rulers and the power of the government." In order to propose a new authority for the foundation of government, Adams must first disprove existing sources of authority.

Argument Two

The second argument states: "Adams appeals directly to his fellow Americans' reason in making his arguments for a republican government." This argument presents Adams's proposal for a new source of a government's authority, the people's ability to reason.

making his arguments for a republican government. He says the US government is founded on the "simple principles of nature."[2] This line of argument invites readers to believe Adams's preferred form of government is logically best because it is derived directly from nature. This allows for a strong foundation of government because it comes from the "natural authority of the people" rather than being imposed on the people.[3]

Adams bases his arguments on the principles of the Enlightenment, which applied human reason to all aspects of society. The cultural movement known as the Enlightenment led to both the French and American Revolutions. The Enlightenment's philosophies also served as the foundation for many of the new political concepts presented in both the Declaration of Independence and the Constitution.

Specifically, the Enlightenment relied on human reason to create a perfect society. According to

Argument Three

In the third argument, the author states: "Adams bases his arguments on the principles of the Enlightenment, which applied human reason to all aspects of society." Because this argument requires background information on the Enlightenment, the author uses two paragraphs: the first provides necessary background information and the second asserts the argument.

Adams, the republican government of the United
States was "contrived merely by the use of reason
and the senses."[4] Building upon this foundation,
the government would not be subject to the abuses
found in many monarchies with power based upon
divine right.

Adams gives his arguments
additional authority by invoking
the Roman philosophers Tacitus
and Cicero. The works of
ancient philosophers provided a
foundation for the ideas of the
Enlightenment. In the preface,
Adams uses the philosophers'
authority to reinforce the
ideals of the Constitution. He
interprets the Roman philosopher Tacitus's text
as support for a balanced government with three
branches to reaffirm his argument. He then uses
three long quotes by Cicero to demonstrate that the
philosopher would support a balanced republican
government. He finishes his appeal to the authority
of the Roman philosophers by arguing that, if they
were alive, they would have thought the Americans
ridiculous if they did not create a better kind of

> **Argument Four**
>
> The fourth argument states:
> "Adams gives his arguments
> additional authority
> by invoking the Roman
> philosophers Tacitus and
> Cicero." This argument shows
> Adams still relies on an expert
> authority beyond himself
> to argue for a republican
> government.

republic based on what they had experienced with Great Britain.

Adams believed in the republican government formed by the US Constitution because it was based on human reason instead of divine right. In the preface to his book *A Defence of the Constitutions of Government of the United States of America*, he argues that divine right was a means of coercion of a nation's citizens, while a government based on reason was founded on the intelligence of the citizens. He appeals to Enlightenment ideas and ancient Roman philosophers in support of his arguments. In a revolutionary time, Adams chose to break away from traditional authority and embrace Enlightenment ideals in hopes of creating a better society.

Conclusion

The last paragraph of the critique serves as a conclusion. Every sentence reviews one of the main points of the essay, relating each point back to the thesis. The final sentence of the paragraph restates and expands upon the thesis.

Thinking Critically about the Preface to *A Defence of the Constitutions of Government of the United States of America*

Now it is your turn to assess the critique. Consider these questions:

1. The description of religious criticism before the critique asserts that humans need academic and spiritual growth. Do you agree or disagree with this concept? Why?

2. Sometimes arguments require the use of context in order to explain the significance of a particular work. How does the information on the Enlightenment expand your understanding of Adams's arguments?

3. A conclusion should summarize the thesis statements and arguments of a critique. It should also leave the reader with a new idea. Is this conclusion effective? Why or why not?

Other Approaches

This critique provides one way to apply religious criticism to the source document. Other critiques might focus on particular aspects of the preface rather than the whole. Another method might focus on the difference between divine right and the religion it is based on. Yet another method could examine how religion in Adams's culture had such a strong influence that he used religious language in his arguments even while promoting authority based on reason.

Grounded in Religion

Another approach to this work could address the apparent contradiction that while Adams rejects divine right to establish government, he believes religion creates the morality necessary for a strong nation. This essay could focus on this excerpt from the preface: "It can no longer be called in question, whether authority in magistrates, and obedience of citizens, can be grounded on reason, morality, and the Christian religion."[5] The thesis might state: Though Adams rejects the principle of divine right, he believes in the necessity of religion to uphold the new US government.

Cultural Religion

Religious language has always been part of public discourse, and Adams's writings were no exception. His works often use religious language and ideas. In his inaugural address, for example, Adams uses a benediction at the end to ask for God's "blessing upon this nation and its Government."[6] One example from his preface to his *Defence of the Constitutions* is that Adams calls the nation "sovereign" and implies that it can be eternal if it stays true to its checks and balances.[7] One thesis for this approach would be: Adams appeals to the philosophy of the Enlightenment, but he uses religious language to describe political reasoning because of the religious influences in his culture.

Adams was elected as the second president of the United States following his time as George Washington's vice president.

An Overview of Adams's Inaugural Address

Historical Context

When popular first president George Washington voluntarily stepped down, the nation was worried. The people would need to elect a new leader, and the political parties that had developed after Washington became president created divisions in the nation. Although Adams had served as Washington's vice president for two terms, the presidential race was close and intense. Jefferson ran for the Democratic-Republican Party and Adams was the Federalist Party candidate. Adams was elected by a mere three electoral votes, securing 71 votes to Jefferson's 68 votes. After such a close election, Adams needed to demonstrate his commitment to the Constitution and Washington's values. He gave his inaugural address on March 4, 1797.

Creation of the Constitution

Adams begins his speech by remembering the American Revolution. He recollects how the colonists felt they had only two options: "unlimited submission" to Great Britain or "total independence."[1] The colonists chose independence because they wanted a new government.

Adams next reminds his listeners of the Articles of Confederation, a document and system of government put in place before the Constitution was created. While the Articles of Confederation failed to unite the states and promote commerce and the freedom of religion, the Constitution of the United States guaranteed the freedom and equality the nation needed to thrive. To enforce this concept, Adams quotes the famous words from the introduction to the Constitution: "to form a more perfect union, establish justice, insure domestic tranquility, provide for the common defense, promote the general welfare, and secure the blessings of liberty."[2]

Praising the Constitution

Next, Adams relates his experience reading the Constitution while living in Europe. He sees the

Constitution "as the result of good heads prompted by good hearts" and states he "did not hesitate" to give it his approval and never "entertained a thought of promoting any alteration in it."[3] Adams goes on to praise the Constitution as a document written by men who represent a nation of high moral character, intelligence, and prosperity. He states he cannot imagine any better government existing than the one outlined in the Constitution, where men are elected by their neighbors. Because of this, he gives his personal stamp of approval to the Constitution. Still, Adams does warn that the US government will fall apart if the elections are not free but are swayed by a political party or the influence of a foreign country.

After this warning, Adams applauds Washington's work as president and upholder of the US Constitution. He hopes Washington will be content with the great part he played in establishing the nation. He holds Washington up as an example to which all future presidents should aspire. Furthermore, he believes Washington should be held up for "the imitation of his successors," all of the elected officials and citizens of the United States.[4]

In his inaugural address, Adams holds up Washington as a figure to be admired and imitated.

Constitutional Candidate

In the last part of his speech, Adams lists his qualifications for taking over the office of president and protector of the Constitution. This personal résumé for president is a sentence 737 words long that includes more than 15 qualities that make him suited for the job. Adams first relates how he intends to support the Constitution, the government it created, and the state governments with their own constitutions. Then he moves on to his qualifications. The first qualification he mentions is "a preference . . . of a free republican government." The second qualification he adds is "an attachment to the Constitution of the United States, and a conscientious determination to support it." He then relates his commitment to furthering the prosperity of the United States through supporting just laws, higher education, the economy, and peaceful relations with the Native Americans. Next, Adams focuses on his commitment to peaceful relationships with other countries. Finally, Adams asserts that he has "an unshakeable confidence in the honor, spirit, and resources of the American people."[5]

Adams concludes his speech with a benediction. He calls on the "Being who is supreme over all" to continue blessing the people and the government of the United States of America with success.[6] This kind of blessing was a common practice at the end of a ceremony or speech during Adams's lifetime. The benediction combined both the earthly and religious authorities to support him in his presidency.

Essential Critiques

Adams stands to the right of Washington, *center*, during Washington's inauguration as president of the United States.

How to Apply Rhetorical Criticism to Adams's Inaugural Address

What Is Rhetorical Criticism?

Careful speakers use the tools of rhetoric to make their arguments stronger. Rhetorical criticism focuses on if and how the words of the speaker or writer have their desired effect upon the audience. Rhetorical critics examine the structure and persuasive techniques of a work to determine why they enjoyed it or felt moved to action by it. By understanding these techniques, critics can improve their own communication skills and recognize when they are being persuaded by a work and why it affects their opinions.

The Greek philosopher Aristotle studied rhetoric and outlined three categories of persuasion, which he called appeals. The first, ethos, is defined as an author or speaker trying to gain an audience's respect by establishing her or his authority on a subject. The second appeal, pathos, refers to an author's attempt to influence the listener's or reader's emotions by using imagery or emotional language. The final appeal, logos, refers to an author presenting an argument in a logical way, giving clear, logical examples that support the claim. Works often use all three of these appeals to some degree. However, they will usually depend more heavily on one of the three.

A speaker may also take advantage of *kairos*, which is the opportune occasion for a speech. The speaker takes into account the opportunities of the particular time and place as well as the constraints on what is appropriate to say, given the circumstances. The speaker also takes the audience into account when making these considerations.

Applying Rhetorical Criticism to Adams's Inaugural Address

Adams had much to prove as he took office, and it was essential his inauguration speech inspire the country's confidence in him. When Adams was sworn into office on March 4, 1797, he stepped into the shadow of the first president, George Washington.

On top of this, Adams was a Federalist, a member of the political party most aligned with Great Britain. He was also the first US ambassador to the British court. His time spent in Great Britain and other parts of Europe earned him a reputation — much proclaimed by the Democratic-Republican Party — of being sympathetic to monarchists. Despite the Democratic-Republican press's attempt to massacre Adams's reputation, the Federalist won the election. After his close victory over Thomas Jefferson, Adams needed to unite the country under his leadership through his inaugural address. He used the opportunity presented by his inauguration as president to make his speech to its greatest effect. Adams's inaugural address uses ethos and pathos to establish his credibility and appeal to his audience's pride in order to convince them that they elected the right man to become the second president of the United States.

Adams begins his speech using ethos by reminding his

Thesis Statement
The thesis statement reads: "Adams's inaugural address uses ethos and pathos to establish his credibility and appeal to his audience's pride in order to convince them that they elected the right man to become the second president of the United States." This essay will focus on how the use of appeals to authority and emotion can persuade an audience.

Argument One

The author begins with the argument: "Adams begins his speech using ethos by reminding his audience of his part in their revolutionary past in order to establish his credibility." This argument contains an appeal asserting Adams's authority in government through his participation in the American Revolution and his prior experience in government.

audience of his part in their revolutionary past in order to establish his credibility. Although Adams never explicitly mentions himself, his references to declaring independence and forming a new government would have brought to mind his role in the revolution. From his initial opposition to the Stamp Act to his participation in the Continental Congress, Adams was a driving force for independence. This background, as well as his service as vice president, establishes his authority in matters of government.

By bringing to mind the actions he took against the injustices Great Britain visited on the colonies, he also disproves the opposing party's claims that he is sympathetic with monarchists.

Adams then appeals to his audience's emotions through pathos by associating himself with their fond memories of

Argument Two

The second argument states: "Adams then appeals to his audience's emotions through pathos by associating himself with their fond memories of Washington." This argument describes how Adams has followed and will continue to uphold Washington's legacy, associating himself with his beloved predecessor.

Washington. Washington was a favorite among the citizens of the United States, having led them in the revolution, the formation of a new government, and the infancy of the new nation. Adams, on the other hand, was often considered unpopular. His personality put many people off. As he later described in a letter to Timothy Pickering, "I am obnoxious, suspected, and unpopular."[1] Despite his dedication to the country, he also reminded people too much of their colonial past and their connection with Great Britain. For example, he supported calling the president "His Majesty the President," rather than the simpler title eventually adopted, "Mr. President."

In order to forestall any negative feelings, Adams first reminds the audience he did not take the presidency from Washington, calling Washington's retirement "his voluntary choice."[2] Then Adams assures his audience that Washington is to be held up as an example to be imitated. This kind of praise seeks to establish that Adams is not becoming president to undo all of Washington's accomplishments but rather to uphold them. This would have been a strong recommendation for Adams's presidency to people who had lived under President Washington.

Argument Three

The third argument states:
"Establishing his credibility
through his history and his
dedication to upholding
Washington's accomplishments,
Adams focuses on an appeal
to the country's pride." In this
argument, Adams reaffirms his
dedication to the Constitution
and his pride in the United
States.

Establishing his credibility through his history and his dedication to upholding Washington's accomplishments, Adams focuses on an appeal to the country's pride. In recalling his first reading of the Constitution while living overseas, he gives his wholehearted approval to the document and the government it creates, which he describes as the best in the world. He finishes his speech with a list of his own qualifications for presidency that relate to his support of the Constitution, including "an attachment to the Constitution of the United States, and a conscientious determination to support it."[3] His detractors might have led some in his audience to worry that Adams, as a Federalist, would seek to establish a strong central government too much like a monarchy. However, his strongly stated approval of the Constitution counteracted these fears.

Adams continues the appeal of pathos by applauding the American spirit. He believes it is acceptable to take pride where it is founded

in "innocence, information, and benevolence."[4] Then, in his list of qualifications to be president, Adams touches on the sources of the country's pride. He reminds Americans he supports the education system and wants to improve the already established manufacturing, agriculture, and commercial industries. He touches on the United States's support of justice both in the country and throughout the world. Finally, he reasserts his belief in the spirit, knowledge, principles, and religion

Adams expresses his deep love for the Constitution in his inaugural address.

of the American people. Rather than truly giving a list of his qualifications, Adams is commending the values and principles of the nation, and then claiming to support each of them himself. Adams is asserting that the United States is great, and as president, he will push it to become even greater.

Conclusion

The last paragraph of the critique serves as a conclusion. The first sentence of this paragraph restates the thesis. The rest of the paragraph continues to summarize the main points of the essay.

Through his inaugural address, Adams sought to win over the hearts of the citizens of the United States by persuading them he was the right man to become their second president. Despite the shadows of Washington's departure and Adams's time spent with the British monarchy, his appeals to authority and emotion established him as a true patriot. He used his own history with the revolution and his support of Washington's legacy to establish his credibility. He then held up his love and support of the Constitution and the American spirit to appeal to the pride of those listening. This speech presented Adams as a strong successor to Washington's legacy.

Thinking Critically about Adams's Inaugural Address

Now it is your turn to assess the critique. Think about these questions:

1. The thesis statement assumes the purpose of the speech was to persuade the audience Adams was the right person to become the second president. What other purpose could his speech have?

2. Another method of persuasive speech is to present a logical argument. Identify a part of the speech that presents a logical argument and explain how it accomplishes this appeal.

3. Select which argument in the critique you felt was the strongest and which you felt was the weakest. Explain your choices.

Other Approaches

This essay represents only one way of applying rhetorical criticism to Adams's inaugural address. But there are countless other ways to apply rhetorical criticism to a speech. Another approach might focus on Adams's audience and their reaction to his speech. A rhetorical criticism could also focus on the longest sentence used in any US president's inaugural address and how Adams used its structure to add to its overall meaning.

Audience Participation

Part of rhetorical criticism looks beyond the speaker to the audience in order to determine how the speech's message was received. Adams had the difficult task of convincing his audience he was a worthy successor to Washington. In his speech, he appeals to patriotic ideals in order to find common ground with his listeners. A critique could focus on the intended audience and its reaction to his speech.

A thesis for this type of critique might state: Adams's speech appealed to the qualities he shared with the audience to convince them of his qualifications for the position of president.

A Sentence to the Purpose

Adams's inaugural address is notorious for its 737-word sentence. This is an unusually long sentence, and many historians believe Adams had a reason for choosing to use this technique. Another rhetorical approach could look at the structure of this long sentence and how Adams used the sheer length of the sentence to portray his own education.

An example thesis for this kind of critique might state: Adams's sentence listing his qualifications for president adds another qualification through its epic length and complicated structure: the authority of his higher education.

Adams, *center*, and Jefferson, *right*, played key roles in the writing of the Declaration of Independence.

9

An Overview of Adams's Letter on Thomas Jefferson

Historical Context

On August 6, 1822, Adams wrote a letter to address a request he had received from Timothy Pickering, a congressman from Massachusetts. Pickering asked him to describe the circumstances surrounding the writing of the Declaration of Independence. Pickering had served as secretary of state while Adams was president. Pickering's political career was turbulent and he was known for his extreme political beliefs. When he retired from politics, he began collecting documentation to write a history of the American Revolution but did not live to see it finished. It is likely Pickering was interested in Adams's account of the writing of the Declaration of Independence to provide supporting documents for his historical work. This letter gives

Timothy Pickering's letter prompted Adams to reveal details about the writing of the Declaration of Independence he had not shared before.

Adams's most detailed account of the creation of the Declaration of Independence.

Advice Given and Followed

Adams begins by recounting the trip from Boston to Philadelphia to attend the Second Continental Congress. He traveled with fellow delegates Samuel Adams, Thomas Cushing, and Thomas Paine. Upon arriving in Pennsylvania, they met with a few local members of the Sons of Liberty. This was a group dedicated to resisting the British government in the period before the revolution. These men warned the delegates not to speak of declaring independence around Philadelphia. They explained that Boston, the home of the delegates, had experienced more oppression from Great Britain than any of the other colonies. This had stirred up their emotions beyond what the other colonies felt. The Pennsylvanian Sons of Liberty also offered this piece of advice: let Virginia take the lead in all political matters.

Adams thought it wise to follow the advice they received concerning Virginia. Virginians prided themselves on being the first and largest colony. Adams felt the other colonies needed to defer to Virginia to keep that state's delegates agreeing with the idea of the revolution. If Congress lost Virginia, the other colonies probably could not stand against Great Britain. Adams thought this advice gave "a color, complexion, and character, to the whole policy of the United States," even up to the time when he wrote the letter.[1] For example, this advice contributed to Virginian George Washington becoming the general of the colonial army. It also influenced the choice of Virginian Thomas Jefferson to write the Declaration of Independence.

Advice Ignored

Adams admits he did not always follow the advice to keep his revolutionary ideas to himself. When he realized the Second Continental Congress was leaning toward reasoning with Great Britain instead of declaring independence, Adams had to voice his opinion. Adams saw Great Britain as proud, domineering, and full of contempt toward the colonies. In his mind, he had only two options: either going to trial and being convicted for treason or getting the colonies to declare independence from Great Britain.

Adams could not keep his support for declaring independence to himself for long. He does not say to whom he mentioned his opinion, but it soon became the gossip of Philadelphia. The colonists most loyal to Great Britain began tarnishing Adams's reputation. The colonists who quietly supported independence pitied him but did not want to be associated with him. In his letter, Adams describes feeling completely alone and unpopular. He says he had felt the same kind of solitude when he acted as lawyer for the British soldiers during the trial following the Boston Massacre. But as time passed, news from the other colonies showed many people supported Adams's beliefs.

Jefferson Declares

The long introduction provides context. Next, Adams finally focuses on the question Pickering asked about the origins of the Declaration of Independence. Pickering specifically asked why a man as young as Jefferson was chosen as the author of the Declaration of Independence. This selection was partly the result of the tendency to elect Virginians to the leadership roles of the revolution. Another prominent, though older, Virginian, Richard Henry Lee, had been chosen to head the committee to draft the Articles of Confederation.

Although Jefferson was young, Adams thought he was highly qualified to be the author of such an important document. Adams explains Jefferson had a "reputation for literature, science, and a happy talent of composition."[2] These three recommendations, balanced with his ability to be "prompt, frank, explicit, and decisive upon committees," led Adams to vote for Jefferson.[3]

Jefferson was elected to head the committee for writing the Declaration of Independence. Adams received the second highest number of votes, which led to him also being placed on the committee as second in command. When the committee met, they elected to have Adams and Jefferson create a draft of the document declaring independence.

Creating the Declaration

Adams recalls that he and Jefferson met as a subcommittee. He then relates a short dispute over who should actually write the draft. In the argument, Jefferson wanted Adams to write the draft. When Adams refused, he presented three major reasons Jefferson should be the author. First, Jefferson was a Virginian. Second, Adams was unpopular, while Jefferson was respected. Third, Jefferson was a much better writer than Adams. After hearing Adams's arguments, Jefferson consented to write the draft.

After Jefferson wrote the draft, he shared it with Adams before it was presented to the entire committee. Adams was thrilled with the writing style. He approved of what Jefferson wrote about slavery but knew the delegates of the southern colonies would not let that portion pass into the final draft. The only part he disagreed with was Jefferson calling the king of Great Britain a tyrant. Adams believed King George III did not have a

The Declaration of Independence is one of the most important documents in the history of the United States.

tyrannical personality. Instead, he believed the king had not been told the truth about the situation in the colonies. However, Adams chose not to make any changes to the draft. Changes could have been made in the full committee or when presented to the Second Continental Congress. The committee chose to present the draft without changes. The Second Continental Congress cut approximately a quarter of the original draft. Adams was sad some of what he considered the best portions were cut before it was published.

Adams concludes his letter with a short answer to Pickering's comment that the Declaration of Independence did not include new thoughts. He agrees with Pickering that all of the ideas in the Declaration had been debated heavily in the First Continental Congress. He also asserts that "the substance of it" was outlined in a pamphlet written by James Otis and published in Boston before the First Continental Congress was even in session.[4]

Jefferson's Reaction

Both Jefferson and Adams agreed they were part of a committee assigned to write the Declaration, but Adams asserts in his letter that he and Jefferson were chosen by the larger committee to be a part of a subcommittee to do the actual writing of the Declaration. Jefferson disagreed with Adams's account. After hearing of Adams's account of the writing, Jefferson wrote a letter to James Madison in which he denied that any sort of subcommittee ever existed. He recalled that at the meeting of the committee he was unanimously chosen to write the Declaration of Independence. Before he presented his draft to the full committee, he first showed it to Benjamin Franklin and Adams to hear their opinions. They gave Jefferson a few verbal comments. He integrated those changes into the document he presented to the entire committee. Unfortunately, no official documentation exists that supports any details beyond what both Jefferson and Adams agree happened in the main committee.

Jefferson disagreed with Adams's account about the writing of the Declaration of Independence.

10

How to Apply Psychoanalytical Criticism to Adams's Letter on Thomas Jefferson

What Is Psychoanalytical Criticism?

Sigmund Freud pioneered psychoanalysis in the early twentieth century. His concepts serve as a vocabulary for psychoanalytical criticism. Freud's theory revolves around the concept of the unconscious, "the complex of mental activities within an individual that proceed without his awareness."[1] Freud focused on the effect the unconscious has on people's conscious minds. The unconscious manifests itself through the actions of individuals in patterns of behavior. The goal of psychoanalysis is to identify psychological problems, which are called disorders or dysfunctions.

The unconscious uses several defenses to avoid changing destructive behaviors. These include selective perception, selective memory, denial, avoidance, displacement, and projection. Selective perception defends by refusing to acknowledge unpleasant experiences. Selective memory is closely related to selective perception; it functions by blocking or modifying unpleasant memories. Denial is a refusal to believe anything painful happened. Avoidance causes a person to stay away from relationships and situations that might cause pain. Displacement takes the pain from one difficult situation and blames it on another situation. Projection places fault on another person for the pain created by a different situation. A psychoanalytic critic might ask about how a work reflects these unconscious defenses in its author.

Applying Psychoanalytical Criticism to Adams's Letter on Thomas Jefferson

Autobiographical history is subject to the unconscious dysfunctions of the author. As Adams describes the writing of the Declaration of Independence in a letter to Pickering on August 6, 1822, his dysfunctions affect his memories of the event. Presuming that Jefferson's accounts of the events are more accurate, Adams's letter to Pickering shows Adams's unconscious need to change how he was remembered in history. His additions to his account of the writing of the Declaration of Independence can be seen as an unconscious response to the personal attacks and lack of respect he felt from the other delegates in the Second Continental Congress. In Adams's letter, his unconscious need to be respected results in the use of selective memory to place himself in a more prominent role in the writing of the Declaration of Independence.

Adams suffered from a poor reputation and loneliness during the Second Continental Congress. During his journey to Philadelphia for the meeting of the Continental Congress, Adams met with a few members of the Sons of Liberty, a pre-revolutionary anti-British group. They warned Adams he had been called a young lawyer "of no great talents, reputation, or weight."[2] Adams writes

> **Thesis Statement**
> A thesis is the main argument of an essay. This thesis uses several common psychoanalytical terms that are defined in the summary. It argues, "In Adams's letter, his unconscious need to be respected results in the use of selective memory to place himself in a more prominent role in the writing of the Declaration of Independence."

> **Argument One**
> The first argument is: "Adams suffered from a poor reputation and loneliness during the Second Continental Congress." This argument establishes the reasons for Adams's later actions.

to Pickering that he was also considered "personally obnoxious" and "too zealous" by many of the members of the Continental Congress.[3] During the Continental Congress, when it became clear Adams supported declaring independence, the opposition "represented [Adams] as the worst of men."[4] This kind of reputation created a solitary life for Adams. He describes himself as an outcast who "walked the streets of Philadelphia in solitude."[5] This left one of the most famous times of his life an unpleasant experience.

Argument Two

The second argument states: "Adams's account of the writing of the Declaration of Independence has a few small but significant differences from how Jefferson remembers it." This argument presents the conflict that calls Adams's account into question.

Adams's account of the writing of the Declaration of Independence has a few small but significant differences from how Jefferson remembers it. Both Jefferson's and Adams's accounts state they were part of a committee assigned to write the Declaration of Independence. In his letter, Adams presents a different version of events, describing how he and Jefferson were chosen as part of a subcommittee responsible for writing the Declaration. In a letter to Madison, Jefferson denied the subcommittee had existed. He recalled the committee had unanimously chosen him to write the Declaration of Independence. He showed the draft to others and integrated their suggestions into the document he presented to the entire committee, but that was the extent of Adams's involvement. Presuming that Jefferson's memory of the events is more accurate, Adams must have had a reason for presenting a different version of events, whether conscious or unconscious.

Adams's account includes details that paint him in a more prominent role. Although Jefferson does not recall any sort of subcommittee, Adams writes in depth about a conversation he and Jefferson had while meeting in that subcommittee. In the conversation Adams relates, Jefferson attempts to give Adams the honor of writing the Declaration of Independence. It is Adams who insists Jefferson do the writing. Two of the three arguments Adams makes for Jefferson to write the Declaration have nothing to do with Jefferson's merit. Adams says Jefferson should

> **Argument Three**
> The third argument further explains the second argument by stating, "Adams's account includes details that paint him in a more prominent role." This argument offers a potential explanation for the differences between Adams's and Jefferson's accounts.

write it because he is a Virginian, which only relates to where he lives and not to any qualities he possesses. The second reason, that Jefferson should write it because Adams is unpopular, is also based on circumstances, not on Jefferson's qualifications. Only in the third argument does Adams praise Jefferson, saying he should have the job of author because of his ability to write well. These details of the subcommittee meeting set up Adams as a respected and honored member of the revolution.

Why would Adams and Jefferson disagree in their accounts? After Adams had such a dismal experience during the months before the Declaration of Independence was written, Adams's selective memory may have altered his role in drafting the Declaration. According to Freud's theories, when a painful memory surfaces, the unconscious uses its defenses to help the individual cope with the pain. Selective memory is an unconscious defense that changes memories to counteract anything

Argument Four

The fourth argument says, "After Adams had such a dismal experience during the months before the Declaration of Independence was written, Adams's selective memory may have altered his role in drafting the Declaration." This argument takes the information from the previous arguments and applies the psychoanalytical criticism to them.

unpleasant in them. Because Jefferson does not remember the subcommittee meeting taking place, it is possible Adams's unconscious created that memory to mask the painful remembrance of being an outcast during the Second Continental Congress. Adams's account of the writing of the Declaration of Independence defends against the pain of bad memories by creating a more significant role for him.

Adams, *left*, and Jefferson, *right*, remained colleagues and opponents throughout their political careers.

Adams's unconscious desire for more respect may have influenced his memories of the writing of the Declaration of Independence. This would have

Conclusion

The final paragraph is the conclusion. It reviews the main points of the essay and restates the thesis. This conclusion also offers a final thought on how the thesis of the critique related to the life of Adams.

affected what he recounted in his letter to Pickering on August 6, 1822, at the age of 88. Jefferson denied the subcommittee and the conversation Adams recounts from it ever happened. However, the differences in their accounts cannot be attributed to Adams's age, since he had written a similar account of the circumstances almost 20 years earlier. Still, the details Adams added into the subcommittee conversation gave him more respect and honor than he received in Jefferson's recollection. Adams's unconscious may have used the selective memory defense to create a more prominent role for himself in the writing of the Declaration of Independence. Adams would go on to be the main orator in defense of the Declaration of Independence, the country's first ambassador to Great Britain, and the country's second president. However, the evidence of this letter suggests Adams's unconscious desired greater appreciation for his involvement in the revolution.

Think Critically about Adams's Letter on Thomas Jefferson

Now it is your turn to assess the critique. Consider these questions:

1. The arguments of this essay build on each other to support the thesis. Are there any arguments that are unnecessary or could be combined with another? Explain why or why not.

2. Do you agree with the idea that Freud's theory of the unconscious can be applied to writing? Why or why not?

3. The conclusion should restate the thesis and arguments listed in the essay. Does the conclusion do this effectively? Why or why not?

Other Approaches

There is always more than one way to approach a work through the eyes of critical theory. Psychoanalytical theory is rich with ideas and concepts that can be applied to works ranging from letters to speeches to works of art. Freud divided the human mind into three parts: the id, the ego, and the super ego. The id is the term he gave to the unconscious. The ego and the superego are both part of the conscious portion of the mind. The superego represents the way cultural pressures shape the mind. It feels guilty when the mind does not follow society's expectations. The ego tries to keep a balance between the desires of the id and the cultural pressures of the superego. Other psychoanalytical approaches might focus on the concept of the ego or the superego, or on the intersection of all three parts of the mind.

The Ego

Another psychoanalytical criticism could focus on Adams's ego. An ego is considered mature if it can wait for what it wants rather than giving in to the desires of the id. A thesis that applies this understanding to Adams's letter might state: In the events described in his letter to Timothy Pickering,

Adams demonstrates a mature ego by giving up the praise of his peers for the greater good of the future revolution by allowing Jefferson to write the Declaration of Independence.

Psychoanalysis and Colonial Culture

A third approach to this letter could use psychoanalysis to understand the culture in which Adams lived. Literary critic Lois Tyson asserts "the relationships among ego, id, and superego tell us as much about our culture as they do about ourselves."[6] This idea can be applied to the events portrayed in Adams's letter to Pickering.

A thesis that applies this concept to Adams might state: The pressure from the British government to submit to their rule creates a longing in Adams's subconscious for independence that he cannot suppress despite his superego's desire to agree with his fellow delegates in the Second Continental Congress.

You Critique It

Now that you have learned about different critical theories and how to apply them to different works, are you ready to perform your own critique? You have read that this type of evaluation can help you look at books, speeches, and essays in new ways and make you pay attention to certain issues you may not have otherwise recognized. So, why not use one of the critical theories profiled in this book to consider a fresh take on your favorite work?

First, choose a theory and the work you want to analyze. Remember that the theory is a springboard for asking questions about the work.

Next, write a specific question that relates to the theory you have selected. Then you can form your thesis, which should provide the answer to that question. Your thesis is the most important part of your critique and offers an argument about the work based on the tenets, or beliefs, of the theory you are applying. Recall that the thesis statement typically appears at the very end of the introductory paragraph of your essay. It is usually only one sentence long.

After you have written your thesis, find evidence to back it up. Good places to start are in the work itself or in journals or articles that discuss what other people have said about it. If you are critiquing a speech, you may also want to read about the speaker's life so you can get a sense of what factors may have affected the creation of the speech. This can be especially useful if working within historical or biographical criticism.

Depending on which theory you are applying, you can often find evidence in the work's language, structure, or historical context. You should also explore parts of the work that seem to disprove your thesis and create an argument against them. As you do this, you might want to address what other critics have written about the work. Their quotes may help support your claim.

Before you start analyzing a work, think about the different arguments made in this book. Reflect on how evidence supporting the thesis was presented. Did you find that some of the techniques used to back up the arguments were more convincing than others? Try these methods as you prove your thesis in your own critique.

When you are finished writing your critique, read it over carefully. Is your thesis statement understandable? Do the supporting arguments flow logically, with the topic of each paragraph clearly stated? Can you add any information that would present your readers with a stronger argument in favor of your thesis? Were you able to use quotes from the work, as well as from other critics, to enhance your ideas?

Did you see the work in a new light?

Timeline

1735 On October 30, John Adams is born in Braintree, Massachusetts, to parents John and Susanna.

1755 Adams attends Harvard University.

1758 Adams begins a law practice in Boston.

1780 Adams authors the Massachusetts Constitution, which serves as a model for other state constitutions and the future Constitution of the United States.

1785 Adams is chosen as the first American ambassador to England.

1787 *A Defence of the Constitutions of Government of the United States of America* is published.

1789 Adams becomes the first vice president, serving under George Washington.

1796 Adams defeats Thomas Jefferson by three electoral votes to become the second president of the United States.

1800 Jefferson defeats Adams for a second term as president.

1764 On October 25, Adams marries Abigail Smith.

1765 In response to the Stamp Act, Adams writes A *Dissertation on the Canon and Feudal Law.*

1767 Adams leads the opposition to the Townshend Acts.

1770 In the trial of the Boston Massacre, Adams defends British soldiers accused of shooting civilians.

1774 Adams attends the First Continental Congress.

1775 Adams attends the Second Continental Congress.

1776 The Second Continental Congress adopts the Declaration of Independence.

1826 Adams dies on July 4, the fiftieth anniversary of the Declaration of Independence.

Glossary

alliance

A union of two or more nations for a common interest.

benediction

A short blessing at the end of a ceremony.

checks and balances

A method of equalizing the distribution of control within a government.

constitution

Foundational laws that establish the rights of the people.

credibility

The quality or power of inspiring belief.

democracy

A government ruled by the people.

divine right

The belief that a god or gods chose a man or group of men to govern a nation.

dysfunction

An unhealthy behavior or interaction within a group.

electoral vote

A ballot cast by a member of the Electoral College, the body of individuals that votes to choose the president and vice president.

psychoanalysis

A method of examining and treating disorders of the mind.

reconciliation

>A restoration of a happy and beneficial relationship.

republic

>A government with an elected president and elected body of representatives to establish laws.

rhetoric

>Effective writing or speaking.

stereotype

>An assumption of a general pattern of behavior.

suffrage

>The right to vote.

Bibliography of Works and Criticism

Important Works

A Dissertation on the Canon and Feudal Law, 1765

Thoughts on Government: Applicable to the Present State of the American Colonies, 1776

Observations on the Commerce of the American States with Europe and the West Indies, 1783

History of a Dispute with America, from its Origins in 1754. Written in 1774, 1784

A Defence of the Constitutions of Government of the United States of America, 1787

Discourses on Davila, 1805

Diary of John Adams, 1856

Autobiography, 1856

Adams Family Correspondence, 1963–1993

The Book of Abigail and John: Selected Letters of the Adams Family, 1762–1784, 1975

Critical Discussions

Dunn, Susan, ed. *Something That Will Surprise the World: The Essential Writings of the Founding Fathers*. New York: Basic, 2006. Print.

McCullough, David. *John Adams*. New York: Simon, 2001. Print.

Miroff, Bruce. "John Adams: Merit, Fame, and Political Leadership." *Journal of Politics* 48.1 (1986): 116. *Academic Search Premier*. Web. 30 Apr. 2012.

Paynter, John E. "The Rhetorical Design of John Adams' Defence of the Constitutions Of . . . America." *Review Of Politics* 58.3 (1996): 531. *Academic Search Premier*. Web. 30 Apr. 2012.

Tyson, Lois. *Critical Theory Today: A User-Friendly Guide*. New York: Garland, 1999. Print.

Resources

Selected Bibliography

Adams, John. *A Defence of the Constitutions of the United States of America*. Philadelphia, 1797. Print.

Adams, John. *Papers of John Adams*. Ed. Robert J. Taylor et al. Cambridge, MA: Belknap, 1977. Print.

Adams, John. *The Works of John Adams*. Ed. Charles Francis Adams. Boston: Little, 1856. Print.

Adams Family Papers: An Electronic Archive. Massachusetts Historical Society, n.d. Web. 20 Aug. 2012.

Hogan, Margaret A., and C. James Taylor, ed. *My Dearest Friend: Letters of Abigail and John Adams*. Cambridge, MA: Belknap, 2007. Print.

Further Readings

Ellis, Joseph J. *First Family: Abigail and John Adams*. New York: Vintage, 2011. Print.

Zall, Paul, ed. *Adams on Adams*. Lexington: UP of Kentucky, 2004. Print.

Web Links

To learn more about critiquing the works of John Adams, visit ABDO Publishing Company online at **www.abdopublishing.com**. Web sites about the works of John Adams are featured on our Book Links page. These links are routinely monitored and updated to provide the most current information available.

For More Information

The Freedom Trail Foundation
99 Chauncy Street, Suite 401, Boston, MA 02111
617-357-8300
www.freedomtrail.org

The Freedom Trail Foundation provides education about the American Revolution in Boston. The Freedom Trail is a brick trail through the streets of Boston that leads visitors to 16 American Revolution historic sites. The Freedom Trail Web site offers a virtual tour of the sites.

Massachusetts Historical Society
1154 Boylston Street, Boston, MA 02215-3695
617-536-1608
www.masshist.org/adams

The Massachusetts Historical Society has archives of Adams family manuscripts that can be accessed online or in person.

Source Notes

Chapter 1. Introduction to Critiques
None.

Chapter 2. A Closer Look at John Adams
1. David McCullough. *John Adams*. New York: Simon, 2001. Print. 144.

Chapter 3. An Overview of Adams's Writings on Women's Right to Vote
1. "Letter from Abigail Adams to John Adams, 31 March–5 April 1776." *Adams Family Papers: An Electronic Archive*. Massachusetts Historical Society, n.d. Web. 19 Sept. 2012.
2. Ibid.
3. Ibid.
4. Ibid.
5. Ibid.
6. "Letter from John Adams to Abigail Adams, 14 Apr. 1776." *Adams Family Papers: An Electronic Archive*. Massachusetts Historical Society, n.d. Web. 19 Sept. 2012.
7. Ibid.
8. Ibid.
9. "John Adams to James Sullivan, 26 May 1776." *The Founder's Constitution*. U of Chicago P, 1987. Web. 19 Sept. 2012.
10. Ibid.
11. Ibid.
12. Ibid.

Chapter 4. How to Apply Feminist Criticism to Adams's Writings on Women's Right to Vote
1. "John Adams to James Sullivan, 26 May 1776." *The Founder's Constitution*. U of Chicago P, 1987. Web. 19 Sept. 2012.

2. Ibid.

3. Margaret A. Hogan and C. James Taylor, eds. *My Dearest Friend: Letters of Abigail and John Adams*. Cambridge, MA: Belknap, 2007. Print. 232.

4. Ibid. xiii.

5. David McCullough. *John Adams*. New York: Simon, 2001. Print. 148.

6. "John Adams to James Sullivan, 26 May 1776." *The Founder's Constitution*. U of Chicago P, 1987. Web. 19 Sept. 2012.

7. "Letter from Abigail Adams to John Adams, 31 March–5 Apr. 1776." *Adams Family Papers: An Electronic Archive*. Massachusetts Historical Society, n.d. Web. 19 Sept. 2012.

8. "Letter from John Adams to Abigail Adams, 14 Apr. 1776." *Adams Family Papers: An Electronic Archive*. Massachusetts Historical Society, n.d. Web. 19 Sept. 2012.

Chapter 5. An Overview of the Preface to *A Defence of the Constitutions of Government of the United States of America*

1. John Adams. "Preface." *A Defence of the Constitutions of the United States of America: Against the Attack of M. Turgot in His Letter to Dr. Price, Dates the Twenty-second Day of March, 1778*. Philadelphia, PA: 1797. Print. iii.

2. Ibid. x.

3. Ibid. xiv.

4. Ibid. xv.

5. Ibid. xvii.

Chapter 6. How to Apply Religious Criticism to the Preface to *A Defence of the Constitutions of Government of the United States of America*

1. John Adams. "Preface." *A Defence of the Constitutions of the United States of America: Against the Attack of*

Source Notes Continued

M. Turgot in His Letter to Dr. Price, Dates the Twenty-second Day of March, 1778. Philadelphia, PA: 1797. Print. xv.

2. Ibid. xiii.

3. Ibid. xv.

4. Ibid. xiii.

5. Ibid. xv.

6. *Inaugural Addresses of the Presidents of the United States.* Washington, DC: US Government Printing Office, 1989. *Bartleby.com.* Web. 19 Sept. 2012.

7. John Adams. "Preface." *A Defence of the Constitutions of the United States of America: Against the Attack of M. Turgot in His Letter to Dr. Price, Dates the Twenty-second Day of March, 1778.* Philadelphia, PA: 1797. Print. xix.

Chapter 7. An Overview of Adams's Inaugural Address

1. *Inaugural Addresses of the Presidents of the United States.* Washington, DC: US Government Printing Office, 1989. *Bartleby.com.* Web. 19 Sept. 2012.

2. Ibid.

3. Ibid.

4. Ibid.

5. Ibid.

6. Ibid.

Chapter 8. How to Apply Rhetorical Criticism to Adams's Inaugural Address

1. Charles Francis Adams. *The Works of John Adams, Second President of the United States.* Boston: Little, 1865. 514. *Google Book Search.* Web. 19 Sept. 2012.

2. *Inaugural Addresses of the Presidents of the United States.* Washington, DC: US Government Printing Office, 1989. *Bartleby.com.* Web. 19 Sept. 2012.

3. Ibid.

4. Ibid.

Chapter 9. An Overview of Adams's Letter on Thomas Jefferson

1. Charles Francis Adams. *The Works of John Adams, Second President of the United States*. Boston: Little, 1865. 513. *Google Book Search*. Web. 19 Sept. 2012.

2. Ibid.

3. Ibid.

4. Ibid. 514.

Chapter 10. How to Apply Psychoanalytical Criticism to Adams's Letter on Thomas Jefferson

1. "Unconscious." *Encyclopædia Britannica*. Encyclopædia Britannica, 2012. Web. 19 Sept. 2012.

2. Charles Francis Adams. *The Works of John Adams, Second President of the United States*. Boston: Little, 1865. 512. *Google Book Search*. Web. 19 Sept. 2012.

3. Ibid.

4. Ibid.

5. Ibid.

6. Lois Tyson. *Critical Theory Today: A User-Friendly Guide*. New York: Garland, 1999. Print. 27–28.

Index

About the Author

Maggie Combs is a freelance writer. She writes mostly in the literary and historical education genres. Maggie lives in Minnesota with her husband, toddler son, and cat. She enjoys time at her cabin and interior design.

Photo Credits

AP Images, cover, 3, 24; Library of Congress, 12, 17, 56, 60, 76, 98, 99 (bottom); North Wind/North Wind Picture Archives, 20, 28, 62; North Wind/North Wind Picture Archives, 28; Bettman/Corbis/AP Images, 38, 45, 46, 84; Scott Rothstein/Shutterstock Images, 69; Victorian Traditions/Shutterstock Images, 74; Susan Law Cain/Shutterstock Images, 81, 99 (top); Augustus Tholey/Library of Congress, 91

3 1333 04082 7022